When an atheist says bless you

Paul Jolly

Fernwood
PRESS

When an atheist says bless you

Fernwood Press
Newberg, Oregon
www.fernwoodpress.com

Cover image: Joanna Axtmann, "Home?ward", 2020, mm, private
collection. Website: joannaaxtmann.com

Printed in the United States of America

ISBN 978-1-59498-071-8

For Anna
Still. Again.

Contents

Fourth orbit

Origins

First spin

Elementary school orchestra miracle

The school takes two weeks (annual schedule
fiasco) to assemble this motley mob of kiddos
in the multi-purpose room. The parents take
two weeks to get signatures (plus ketchup smudges
and baby erp) on permission forms. The district

takes two weeks to truck brass and woodwinds,
warehouse to school (including a delay while twelve harps
are strung, tuned, misdelivered, and returned).
You have November (minus Thanksgiving) and half of December
to replace that motley mob of lip buzzers and frictionators

with a standing-O-worthy ensemble. The ersatz horsetail
catgut contraptions have no frets, so kiddos guess
the tones, natural, sharp, flat. The lip
buzzers wince from the cheek muscle ache.
Plus, the kiddos have to learn to read birds-

on-phone-wire notation at the same time that they learn
the contraptions. Plus, speed and loudness clues
are in Italian. But you knew the job impossible when you took it.
Parents will help on the standing O. Like their winter
concert seats are spring loaded to hoist

their bottoms into the air. Like their phone cameras were built
to capture this moment: lighting perfect, zoom
in on the specific kiddo, audio symphony quality.
Now it's second day orchestra rehearsal. Homework
for lip buzzers was a thirty-second tongueless

raspberry. Homework for frictionators was drag bow
across an open string up and down,
same speed. You stand at the podium and lift
your baton. Do the miracle—Jingle Bells
in six weeks—one more time, God willing.

When an atheist says bless you

An atheist's sneeze propels phlegm
flecks ninety miles an hour.
A soul fragment surfs each fleck.
Tissue's purpose is collect phlegm.

Bless you's purpose is collect soul fragments.
Burps, flatules, coughs, tears,
other body emits generate a glare.
Only sneeze gets blessed. The words

bless you get ejected with the same reflex
as sneeze. All angels who hear dispatch,
bitty cute cherubim and muscular
seraphim, descend the pole and board

the bless-truck. Trinkets of blessing: sidewalk
nickel, New Orleans Mardi Gras
beads, rainbow sticker, cheap
as Cracker Jack prizes. Proud angels

used to frown at atheist sneeze
bless. Work is scarce now. Any task
beats sit, listen to dispatch
blather. The mutual recoil of atheist

blesser and desk angel masked
in bland script: All angels are assisting
other blessers. Are you willing to complete
a survey at the end of this call?

Queen Victoria's reading list

The untrue vignette rolls generation
to steeper generation propelled
by the tasty image that stiff-spined
baffled servants delivered the math treatise
to her majesty. It doesn't matter that the queen
never dreamed of an integer
on a toadstool smoking a hookah.

We don't care that she didn't imagine
a hypotenuse and a hippopotamus
dancing together at the Lobster Quadrille.

She might as well have chuckled
in the middle of a full-starch state dinner
secretly wondering if the Cheshire cat
sat on a log or a logarithm
as it became negative cat.

If she had complained to the royal
physician, trusted guarantor
of the fiction of monarchy,
he might have prescribed a bottle
labeled "Drink Me" with no clue
he compounded her nightmare.

The birds and the bees

In the beginning was one bird,
one bee. He admired her wasp
waist. She longed to nest in his pec
feathers. He resisted the urge to bite
her in half, snack on thorax, save
abdomen for later. She mused:
a sting to the heart could kill
him. Awkward silence. Um, now
what? she asked. He didn't know
but felt he should display mastery
of some maneuver. Why do
you eat worms? she asked, sharper
than she meant to. Why do
you fly so funny? he demanded.

Millenia later, there are many millions
of birds and bees. They don't talk
to each other. Cole Porter tinkles
his keys. Croons about love.
The bird/bee alliteration's lovely,
but Cole has no idea what he's singing.

Smart kids

Smart kids don't think, they know.
Smart kids read the quiz while the teacher
starts: "Be..." Correct answers

flood smart heads, cascade down arms,
and pencils fill in blanks when the teacher
says "...gin." They slam

the textbook with a flourish,
swagger, stroll, shuffle to the teacher's
desk, plop down the test, strut back,

slump and pull a sci-fi novel from their backpacks.
Or finish the year's homework.
All the homework. All classes.

I tried the smart kid thing once. Hotwire
the synapses. Eyeball, brain, hand, pencil
all in sync. I doublechecked all ten

answers before I finished reading
question one. I was one hundred percent
sure I got one hundred percent right.

Then, paralysis. What will other kids
think I think of them if I stand?
It's a not-fun fun house hall of mirrors.

What if I fall, swaggering face first to the floor?
I'll fold quiz, paper airplane, and sail it to the teacher's
desk. No, too much chance of a crash. I'll stay

in my seat till the bell rings and drop
the test on the desk with the rest of the hoard
on the way out the door. Or I'll fold test

in book, book in backpack, brain
in daydream, find test at bedtime.
That's the kind of smart kid I am.

If you need anything

The server pours coffee for me and Travis
and says, "My name is Jessica if you need
anything." I tell Travis there's a poem
in the works about a waitress whose name
depends on a customer's needs. "It's been done,"

says Travis. "Half a dozen stand up
comics got there first." In an instant I turn
from a whip smart wit with a wicked comment
plucked from the detritus of strip mall life

into another exploitive dude with notebook
and disposable pen, sipping refills till my hand
shakes. I am a hack in the schmuck-slump

swamp, peering up at the wisdom perch.
But Jessica! Soaring above the mundane
diner scene, whether we want ketchup,
or a peek at the desert menu, or a coffee

top-off, or our check, she stays Jessica, in fact.
Whatever the father and son in the corner
booth want, her Jessica-ness is intact.

Community project

I come bearing only the jeans.
Knees bulge through holes
like an old joke. Someone brings
a patch, an island in search of a sea.
Someone, surely a fencer in a former
life, procures a needle.
The tightrope walker has a foot
of thread. The thimble of course comes
under its own steam, on a one
-inch bicycle, heaving and huffing
after its long climb. We'll begin
as soon as I work up
the nerve to take off my pants.

Church without curses

Christopher Wren, architect of Saint Paul's
Cathedral, forbids laborers from swearing

on site. Anyone heard using the Lord's
name in vain is axed forthwith from payroll.

A mason drops a stone on his foot.
He almost faints but does not cuss.

A foreman finds mortar-mixers napping.
He nudged them awake instead of cursing.

When the glazier slices his hand open,
he grips tight, grunts, but does not blaspheme.

The cathedral takes forty years to build. It might
have been faster, but not without salty vocabulary.

The gold plate could have been slathered on the vaulted
ceiling by a cockney who turned the air blue.

The massive organ pipes could have been clanged together
double-quick, but it would have required coarse language.

Saints statues could have been slapped
onto the roof by a vulgar bloke. It would have shaved

five years off the construction. But when you walk
narthex to altar, you feel the second

commandment honored as each stone
slid to fit tight to stone.

Adam plans a picnic

Adam wants to take Eve on a picnic.
He asks, Are you free for dinner tomorrow?
Sure, she says. What time. He runs away
shamed by his clocklessness.
Adam wants to take Eve on a picnic.
Before picnic, picnic basket. Adam collects
and weaves palm fronds, with a checked gingham
lining. The word gingham makes Eve giggle.

Adam wants to take Eve on a picnic.
The menu starts fancy: pheasant,
chilled leek soup, mincemeat pie. But he settles
for pine nuts and blackberries.

The harrowing terrors of snake, apple, exile
are distant future. He wants to avoid
awkward silence so he practices prompting questions:
Where do you go when you walk for days?

What does God look like to you? Is it right, do you
think, for animal to eat animal? What kind
of creature are you? Your tumbling, roaring, coaxing
beastliness—what is it? What does it want from me?

Heaven forbids me to be proud and presumptuous

I am dogged by an angel squadron whose only goal
is to monitor my ego meter. If my head gets big,
they impose the head cramp clamp. If I get too big
for my britches, they stuff my haunches into smaller britches.

If I climb on my high horse, they put silly plastic tassels
on its ankles. They make sure I don't take undue
credit. Or due credit. An angel is stationed
at every mirror in the house to thwart vanity.

"Move on," he sputters when I admire my dashing
smile. They take me down three peg for every peg
I climb. They crush the air from an overblown self.
But their special vigilance is false modesty. Soon as I lower

myself they crow, "You haven't earned that humility."
Some day I will give them the slip, dive from the window
when they aren't looking. Hitchhike or run. Stop second
guessing every guess, stop strip searching every observation.

Let me be clear. I don't want to be god or saint or angel.
Just a not unhandsome, sometimes funny, middle aged
male specimen of the species. And the writer
of a dozen (lifetime total) poems that melt heaven's gates.

Family of saints

Adalsindis spilled the cornflakes and flogged
his shoulders in penance. Clotsindis found
a love note tucked in the pocket of her backpack
and took an ultra-chastity vow on the spot.
She never in the rest of her life looked
at another male, including father and brothers.
Eusebia was fasting again—Mom called her for breakfast
three times before she remembered. Maurontius
was up all night studying for his theology
test by the light of an angel's hands.
Mom and Dad relented when he craved coffee.

They guzzled a scalding gallon each before rushing
to work. Her: curing the incurables
with intercessory prayer. Him: battling
heathens who threatened the borders
of the recently converted country. In moments of rest
mid-fracas, he scribbled notes for his apologia,
a treatise against heresies.

He refuted the notion that Christ was only human
in a memo he stuffed into the crevice
between breastplate and shoulder plate.
He dispatched the idea that Christ was only divine
in a caustic rebuttal that he stuck in the left
knee joint. And he solved the schism

between Easter-on-Passover believers and Easter
-on-Sunday folks. He scrunched that missive
between chain mail shirt and sweaty chest.

When he unsheathed himself for dinner with the fam,
(meatloaf, mac and cheese) the schism tract
draft was a sweat-smudged mess. He tried to re-catch
his logic. But Rictude, bless her, was yammering
about Eusebia's (bless her, too) endless fast.
Maurontius was sure he'd flunked the exam
because he'd written Hippolitus was pope
and Zephyrinus was anti-pope, or the other way around.
Adalsindis teased Clotsindis about K.I.S.S.I.N.G.
Adalbald, like many fathers before and since, roared
for silence. That roar became The Great Silence,
dripped into the stones of monasteries
throughout Christendom, refuge of all fathers.

Show and tell

The monster owner lugs it to school in a flimsy
wire cage on show and tell day. The monster snores
dis-melodiously in the back of the classroom

during the Pledge of Allegiance. Practices
raspberries while permission
slips for next week's field trip are collected.

Monsterless kids display timid magic tricks.
Common baseball cards. Dumb bottle cap collections.
Boring scout badges. They feel out-classed

but stutter on. Monster's turn. The monster
is learning to talk but stays mum. Allegedly
obeys commands, but rebels today. Is said to know

math but botches one plus one. Monster
farts. Children guffaw. The teacher
whispers, "Put the monster back in the cage."

But of course the monster spread eagles
to avoid reencagement. Of course the monster
diarrheas on the encyclopedias.

And once the class starts roaring, laughter,
fright, disgust, order won't come back. In a few years,
the monster will ring the puberty bell.

The monster will reach the rank
reek and mayhem of teen years.
When the monster is stronger

and heavier than Dad, mischief tilts at a sinister
slant. Meantime, it's milquetoast mishaps.
Caca on the walls. Bellowing during naps.

Exodus from the barbers' union

First the surgeons left the barbers union
to hang their amputate and blood
-let shingles in a tonier part of town.

Then the dentists packed their picks,
pliers, and chisels and harrumphed
out of the guild hall. They claimed

clipped hair swirled into their patients'
propped-open mouths, but the ruse
fooled no one. They wanted to max the lucre.

Now the colorists are collecting their toxic
stains—sword-blade blue for the ancient ladies,
teal for teens, ginger highlights for dirty blondes.

When dyers exit, it will just be the oldster
with his stained apron, mosquito-drone
clippers, cord too short to reach the chair.

He will slouch in the chair himself, wait
for that loyal weekly customer who wants
a touch-up for his hardly longer hair.

But what about Snuffy?

I can't requite your love, but I requite
the squiggly heat of your toaster
and the squeak of your shoes.
I requite the swirl of your cowlick
and the greenness of your potted fern.
Your dachshund and I found requitement
the minute we met. I hope Snuffy
and I can be friends, regardless.

I see you are heartbroke. I know I sent
sixed mignals. I flirted, you loved, your love
was quite, I declined to requite.
Can I bring Snuffy a dog biscuit?

I requite the wealth of your bookshelves,
the shade of your balcony. Your plate
of bacon-wrapped, cream-cheese-stuffed
dates, I would walk across town
for that requitement. You say, It's a no go.
You say go, so I go. I hope, when your heart
normalizes, maybe next week,
maybe joint Snuffy custody.

Clipboard shortage, shared chart

Hospital's short on clipboards, so my roommate's
medical history and mine got smunched onto one chart.

One of us is here for a heart murmur. The heart
swallows its words, fails to project.

The other has a concussion. Bumped his head
and he went to bed and he couldn't get.

One of us is a bile spitting atheist, prone
to retch at the mention of deity, if not full puke.

The other is an unctuous subscriber who summons
a priest to perform last rites—the whole

holy water, rosary, candle, text, and incense
shebang. The priest, a formerly tremulous man,

is resigned to this strange church where each
congregant is marked with a plastic bar

coded wrist strap, where pews are horizontal,
where no one came for the sake of worship.

The priest wants a signal. But one of us naps,
the other is drugged to euphoria. So

he stands in the doorway and prays
quietly to an inoffensive God.

Thank you late comer

You wait in a long Starbucks line
for a double shot caramel skim milk
frappuchino en route to the zendo,

so you arrive after the gong tumbles from hum
to silence. You scrunch your zafu noisily
before settling, like a dog circling

his blanket, into your crooked half-lotus.
A fussy dog. But dogs are punctual.
They don't get tugged off course

by a peripheral glimpse of a Starbucks
logo. See what you've done to me?
Dog, good. You, bad. Dualism, the route

to suffering. You crank the decibels
on my inner corrosive chatterbox. You hold
a mirror to my ugly twisted angry face.

Forgiveness is a spiral road with no radial
shortcuts. You get a caffeine turbo-buzz.
I get this zip of rage. Soon the gong will sound

again, I hope. We will bow to the sensei, shuffle
out the door, you to another damned frappucchino,
me to the rest of my obviously unenlightened life.

The three outrages of Chicken Soup for the Soul dog food

One. A dog won't slurp chicken soup
—too many noodles. Two. A dog has no soul

in any theology, pan, mono, or poly.
Three. A dog might snarf soul food slipped

off the table, fatback scraps or pig feet, but Chicken
Soup for the Soul dog food is such obvious

overreach that any dog lover, clergy or lay,
must see through the ruse. First the book,

heartwarmer, best-seller, spoon-fed spirit pablum
without the chunky superstition trappings.

Then a sequel. Then the sequel's sequel. Book
tours. Talk show bookings. Then notecards

sporting smarmy cheerful quotes. But CS
for the S dog food is a new low in brand

expansion. A new range of MBA zeolotry. A soul
eats no chicken soup. It eats chickens whole,

fresh from head-chop block and feather-pluck
bucket. And a dog eats table scraps or molded

pellets. Sleeps on the floor. Please don't tell
me there's a Chicken Soup for the Soul doggie bed.

Second rotation

Some day of course
the bear himself

The threat of a stung snout is hardly
worth the tongue-scoop of pleasure.
Why should a half ton lunk lurk

hungry, hunt for honey driplets
and trickles when with a few quick
shifts he can manufacture his own?

Damp winglets poke through the shag,
every day more able to thrust his bulk
onto the waiting blanket of summer air.

He has two thirds of the needed legs.
The other two are skeleto-evolutionary
hints, waiting to claim their moment.

Some day the black bear will cavort
down a steep meadow, galumph
skyward, flit rose to honeysuckle,

pad its haunches with bunched pollen,
salute the shapeless queen, and snuggle
into a hexagon with all the other bear bees.

On nudity

You can romp buck naked, goose pimples erect,
but stash your clothes in a box or locker. No priest
wants to skin his shin tripping on a garter
dropped in the monastery garden. Pilgrims crawl
shrineward with shins and elbows
tangled in teddies. It interferes with the pilgrimage
ambiance. The exorcist trots toward the possessed
to evict malevolent spirits. He rehearses
his Latin invectives. He shouldn't have to dodge
thongs that dangle from a branch. The monk
who peers from his tiny cell window
and sees bustiers strewn on the monastery
lawn always relapses to annoyance. Then remorse
for the annoyance. Then he gets mad.
If you just thrust your frilly under layers
into a hedge it would help.

Nudists and clerics can co-exist if we mind
our manners. Lacy things simply do not belong
in the chapel. The abbot long since stopped
droning about the angel at the gate of Paradise,
evicting fig leaf draped Adam and Eve.
He knows some wear floor-length burlap
cinched with rope and some wear oops nada.
He's OK with that. So don't complicate his psalm
singing by flinging underthings in his way. Don't strip
and flaunt where he does his holy spirit jaunt.

Strong adhesive

Good work prompts pride! I know it's just a number
ten envelope, but that envelope may carry a spicy
hot-breath first-love love note. Or a child support
check. Or a clipped obit for the ex who sort of cares.

Some earnest soul will hack up saliva to stick flap
to back. Or (likely) it's "last chance before your bill
is bounced to collection." But you're American.
This is a Yankee Doodle American company.

The whole factory will be bounced to collection
if the adhesive doesn't adhere. And remember the career
ladder. Maybe it's not a minimum wage dead
end gig. You could be promoted to the top

secret ambassador pouch adhesive team. Or the Olympic
sprint shoe sole attach department, where shoddy product
means tread on the track and tears on TV. You could
be deputized to mix glue to hold the star on this year's

Rockefeller Center Xmas tree. Hell, you might meet
Mr. Rockefeller himself. You think Mr. R has no job
for a nose to the grindstone glue mixer? Back
to work. Buck up. Make that flap stick.

Cleanliness

Soap used to clean us. Now it cleanses.
It used to smell nice. Now it blesses
with aromatherapy. Grime, grease,
and funk odor have been banished

from the human body for decades. What frontiers
can soap conquer? One liquid body wash
promises soothing caresses. One pampers
with zen-like bliss, minus years of pondering

koans. The cascade of calming essences
baffles: olive oil, shea butter, grapefruit
seed extract, mango jelly, rose petal distillate.
But watch out. Just as viruses mutate

to survive drugs, new soap-proof breeds
of filth are evolving. Oozes and gunks
no soap can dissolve. This year, this month,
is an apex of human spic, human span.

If cleanliness is next to godliness, we're on a fast
tilt to hell. Foul grunge. Fetid stink. On a bicycle
without brakes, chain grease splashes
our faces as we careen into the damned abyss.

Pop goes the weasel

Everyone blames the primate. "Monkey thought
twas all in fun" sounds so sinister.
But there's no foul play. Why is everyone

in nursery school so quick to whodunnit? Maybe
it's a burst appendix with extra kablooie.
Flinty weasel claws could ignite abdominal

mulberry fumes. Charles Dickens in Bleak House
wrote of spontaneous human combustion, complete
with oily reek and smoke-smudged walls.

Biologists scoffed. But no one disproved spontaneous
weasel combustion. So back off the monkey.
Cancel the inquest. Dismiss the grand jury.

Wipe that smirch off the monkey's besmirched
reputation. It's trauma enough without blame
to see your playmate in flames. He'll go back

to his pack, to grimace and nit-pick grooming.
No more big city thrill. No more penny for a ball
of thread, penny for a needle, free rodent explosion.

Two fish tanks at the Diablo Canyon nuclear power plant visitors center, 1979

Admitted, on a plaque above two fish
tanks in the Diablo Canyon visitor's center: *the nuke
plant will dump hot water in the Pacific. Native fish
will exit for cooler zones. They'll be replaced*

by warm water lovers! Rockfish, crappies, sand
bass exiting the bay will exchange small talk
with tropical exotics like clownfish and angelfish
swimming in. Here begins the big splat migration.

Honey bees, frogs, and most bats migrate
to their reward. Pie in the sky when they die
bye and bye, bye-bye, now. Polar bears, dressed
like gondoliers, shove off the mainland on shrinking

icebergs, seek colder sub-zeros, harder ice, longer
winters. Bad news, bears. You have no destination.
Hardy invasives migrate every which. Roaches,
rats, deer, kudzu, poison ivy: all the survivors

thrive and claim turf. The tender beasts,
uniquely perched in their own patch, watch
that patch shrivel. At the core of every creature's
instinct is this final message: if the life

you know no longer works, vamoose.
Scatter. Somewhere, maybe, is a sheltered
spot where you can rest, replenish, nest,
safe for babies to sleep and suck, sleep and suck.

The flip side

A salesman makes a killing, rushes to cash
his commission check. A customer dies from buyer's
remorse. Obit reads: he loved to shop

Good King Wenceslus is Yankee Doodle
in a minor key. A midwinter dirge and a Fourth
of July jingle poke through the zodiac's

spokes on opposite poles. Every high
altitude kite flier's shoelaces entwine
the whiskers of a morose gopher

who wants to burrow deep. One kid
tugs Mom's sleeve: "Let's go to the park."
A sibling rebels and grumps.

Every slump anchors a mania.
It's a mood-tumble mandala,
a piston stilt pogo stick yo yo

world. When you're in the dumps,
I top euphoria. I salute your good
cheer while a tear drops in my beer.

Post extinction herpetology convention

The annual herpetology convention still convenes
years after the last frog went belly-up extinct.
The agenda is mush. Some papers urge bust
open the cryogenic tadpole bank. Some rugged field

scientists tell of treks that failed to find a live
frog. Some misty-eyed humanists get nostalgic
and idolize the giants from the good old days,
the good old frog days. One crank always opines

about a medieval theory that mud spawns frogs.
Sixth-sense-gadgeteers show slides that capture
murky shadows, so called frog specters. There is always
a workshop for new doctorates with a shiny diploma,

houseworth of debt, god-awful job options. I go
for the screw. My once-a-year fling. A fellow frog
-head from the pre-extinction era, an adjunct prof
with exquisite legs, thrusts toward me, swims upstream.

Meet the Turpitudes

Mama Moral Turpitude is most notorious. Still don't
-caring after all these years. If you say turpitude,
she answers. If you see public displays of adultery,
or tipplers tipping back tumblers, she's involved.

Five year old Hygiene Turpitude—don't ask when he last
brushed his teeth. It's a unitooth now, and the floss-
garotte can't penetrate. The Coca-Cola coating is crusty
crystals. Good news: they fall out by age seven.

Enviro Turpitude slobbers and drips snot in puddles
so his fluids will corrupt a watershed. His pee renders
fish with ova in their testes, sperm in their overies.
He can out-methane-fart a field of cows.

Formal name Military Industrial Turpitude. Everyone
calls him Millin. Ask in a bar what he does, he says arms
smuggler with a straight face. Or mercenary. Or kill.
Or he smiles and says, Water always runs downhill.

If you see them in your neighborhood, don't, please
don't, mount your high horse. The Turpitudes
rally at the sight of a high horse. Campaigns to evict
Turpitudes pump resolve into them like air

into a beachball. They dig in their pointy heels. Tie
hair to fence posts and fortify it with superglue.
Handcuff wrists to doorknocker. Cement feet
to sidewalk. You will lose this fight, Mr. Goody Pants.

All the trees we save

The hemlock muscling into the sky
in the park is all the toilet
paper we save by wiping with recycled
TP instead of virgin wood pulp TP.

The massive oak on the river bank still stands
because Starbucks emails receipts
instead of cluttering pockets with paper scraps.

We like our privacy. Two thirds
of households are unlisted. The phone
book that rots on every porch
is slim, so the hickory in the traffic
circle survives. If the phone company stopped
the annual phone book toss there would be two
hickories in the circle.

Official documents now use commas
instead of dashes. Saves enough paper
to save the ugly shrub in front of town
hall from the shredder.

The council holds a hearing on a proposed
Kleenex ban. If you cry, use a hanky.
The laundry lobby is in favor; the funeral
lobby opposes. Tree lovers hold
signs: Eschew tissues. One angry enviro holds

a photo of the chestnut in his yard
that will be axed if the ban fails. His rant
devolves to spittle, and the guards escort
him out. He sits on the town
hall steps, inhaling deeply the oxygen
plume that billows from every tree in town.

The oozers against the tidies

At the annual poets picnic, we challenge
the body fluid poets to softball. The score
isn't close. Us tidies are efficient

base hitters, occasional grand slammers.
The oozers foul out every time at bat.
Between innings, before we take the dugout,

we squeegee the benches, mop
home plate, hose down the backstop.
The cocktail of spittle, bile, semen, milk

is enough to coat the whole field with slick.
That's even before the bleeding starts!
One runner from the ooze brigade

makes first base. Tries to steal
second, retreats, slips in his mucus
streak. Most tidies never sweat.

We change uniforms when we exude
the first bead. We spend more time
laundering than playing ball.

A poet can keep her secretions secret.
We are not all first responders,
if-it-bleeds-it-leaders, wranglers

at the spread-your-flesh-on-the-table rodeo.
Your ooze is none of my beeswax.
Patch your weepy sores. Bandage

the gape and curtail gangrene. Skin
is a brilliant thing. Keeps insides in.
Makes it possible for a ball team to win.

The lost boy

Mikie grows to six feet, exudes grown man
odors, sprouts chin stubble, but never parks
his lagoon and launches flamingos into the sky.

When Mikie enters a room, the marshy
patches splash a mud splotch on the door
frame. Who'd blame a host who cringes?

He's cute as an overgrown larva that won't metamorph.
Mikie takes a month-or-longer wander,
imposes on Big Sis Wendy: Tend my pet rats.

John lets Kid Bro Mikie borrow his new car.
Mikie is mum when he returns the keys.
Odometer admits two thousand mystery miles.

You think Mikie can slip back to Neverland
long after Wendy and John forget how to fly?
Peter Pan bans Mikie and his damned lagoon.

Mikie has no oomph, no life plan. Pet rats
and lagoon limit his range. Jobs and romances
start and splutter. No rule dooms him to lagoon.

He could land it whatever he chooses.
Many flamingos would proudly call him master,
circle his head, warn him of coming disaster.

Act natural

Place your elbows where relaxed
hombres do. Once you perfect a gesture,
don't overwork it. Master vocal
volume: pianissimo and fortissimo
only hit the mark on the opera stage.

Don't think technique. Take your pocketed
hands out every couple minutes
but don't flap them around like flustered
pigeons. Don't laugh alone. Be
yourself, but emphasize your cool side.

Try to help someone, but keep a low
profile. No one wants to be HELPed.
Don't talk more than a minute
without pausing to see if your audience
is still there. Be brave enough to take

an unpopular stand, but just before
it turns popular. Like liking a hokey
song a week before the curse
of hokeyness lifts. Hum it quietly
so only people who know know you know.

Inside you is a cool kid who knows
when to laugh in scorn, when to laugh
in friendship, when to tip back your head
and laugh with double-lungful abandon.

On witnesses

The dead travel in pairs. They kibitz
and kvetch about our metrics fixations.

Bricklayer ghosts snicker if a mason
(living) drops a plumb line. They joke: these days
builders don't know which way is up.

If you scoop a quarter cup dried parsley
for the soup de jour, the former cooks (deceased)
harrumph, "A good cook invents."

All chemists know measurements matter—live
chemists. Dead chemists loiter
in laboratory corners, discuss catalysts,
reactions, a dash of this, a little of that.

Dead nurses elbow live nurses away from the patient.
"We do dosage by eyeball," they say,
exuding syringe mastery and confidence.

The ghosts in the embalming room scoff
at the mortician's care calibrating embalming
fluid. "Just slosh formaldehyde in the abdominal cavity."

In heaven there are no calipers, no scales,
no yard sticks. When the witnesses come
back to visit, they forget the living rely on ratios.

When the unclean spirit leaves a man

When the unclean spirit leaves a man, it's a church
work day. Children stay up past bedtime the night
before to help plop potluck cookie dough
on cookie sheets and lick the mixing bowl.

The church men are up early, happy to be excused
from Saturday morning Bible study. Know-how
and power tools are hauled out by the pick up truck
load. Three guys bring power vacs. Two bring electric

plumbing snakes. There are five nail guns. If they don't run
a Zamboni-size floor scrubber across the linoleum,
it's because they couldn't squeeze it through the door.
Walls are painted beige. Cracks are caulked. End

of the day, the dumpster bulges with dust bunnies,
pizza boxes, cracked Venetian blinds, ratty carpets,
rats, and booze bottles. The welcome-home
sinner's expected in the front pew next day.

Sunday morning, pastor prays in gratitude for one
soul snatched from Satan's grasp. The home makeover
crew feels pride rise. Meanwhile, exiled devil
returns. What makes you think an unclean

spirit doesn't like a clean house? Evil demons,
turns out, are major league neat freaks. He whistles
to his evil cohort: safe to move back in.
Back slide. Back lash. Whip lash likely.

Learning to wait

This is how we wait, boys
and girls. Arms at your sides.
Bill, hands out of your pockets.
Jim, clock-watching makes

it worse. Jeff, hands out of Jill's
pockets. Spine straight. Don't slump.
Most teachers assert math or English
is the most important hour of the school

day. Kids all claim recess is best. I assert
this moment is key: waiting in line.
History, PE,—the whole school schedule
punctuates waiting. Barb, stop twirling

your hair. Rick, finger out of your nose.
Wayne, stop squirming. Meg, eyes
straight ahead. You can learn more
from the neck of the kid in front of you

than from the scene out the window. When I
was your age, I spent Sunday evenings
in practice to be the erectest, stillest
line-waiter in the Monday morning

line up. In high school, I took intro
to ballet five times to perfect my standing
technique. I was a standing-in-line major
in college. My doctoral thesis was on standing

in line. I knew as soon as I got that diploma
I wanted to help other people learn
to stand in line. If something is worth
having, it's worth standing in line for.

Standing in line purifies your desire
for what you say you want. It filters
the blood, clears the mind of flotsam,
scrubs the lungs, softens the crusty heart.

Brain facts

A brain weighs three pounds.
A brain is three quarters water.
In grade school I learned people use only ten
percent of their brains. So a brain

contains two pounds (that's a quart)
of unused water. All those Hs and Os
loiter on street corners, wait
for trouble, like Jets and Sharks.

The devil finds work for idle
cells. Quick! Name the curling
part of the staple. Remember or invent.
Como se dice en Ingles an ear

wax fetish? Give me a word for the failure
of envelope glue. What do you call
a dream that includes odors that enter
the dreamer's nostrils? How do you measure

the impact of slope on a ricochet's
angle? The impact of bulge? The impact
of impact? Make flash cards. Invent
mnemonic jump rope chants.
Put that sloshing quart to work.

Third cycle

Buffer your circumference

An apple a day keeps the doctor away.
Garlic vexes vampires. The lowly
mushroom keeps circus clowns at bay.
Marshmallows repel air traffic
controllers. Lima beans are reputed
to discourage street corner evangelists.

Homeopaths explain: the tiny essence
of a thing, distilled to within a sliver
of nothing, is its antidote. Alchemists,
cabalists, star readers and dice tossers,
each sect has its own tables of correspondence,
reduce, distill, simile, leap.

Buffer your circumference. Ice
cream sandwiches are proof
against yetis. Grapefruit protects
from bad barbers. Bok choy stops
snake skin booted car salesmen. Fill
your satchel with the right stuff
for safety from all misfortunes.

Help

I call animal control, and a rat shows up:
teeth filed, tail scabbed, claws cracked,
with a toolbox full of mosquitoes.

I call the fire house, and a busload
of arsons appears, each with a pocketful
of flints, each with a tin cup of gasoline.

I call the police to report a prowler.
The same prowler, in the same busted hat,
knocks on my door to offer help.

I blame the switchboard operator
in the basement. No one taught her which jacks
connect to which party line. The long

distance operator laughs at her when she tries
to place a call. She still hopes the big
city will introduce her to Mr. Right,

or her style will be recognized as talent.
But how can that happen when she's stuck
in this basement office, closet really, and her only

friend is the sun that spends an hour
daily traversing the tiny window?
She intuits which jack goes in which socket,

wrong, wrong, wrong, as she counts
how many paychecks till she earns a bus
ticket home, and imagines Dad's hug.

The bridges of Madison County

You said you'd be back by ten from a date
with your soon-to-be-second-husband. You gave
me a book you said would explain your exit.
Five-year-old Evan slept next to me on the couch,

and I turned the pages instead of heaving
the book, over and over. It was a masterwork
of unadulterated schmaltz. The cuckolded
was an Iowa pig farmer who allowed your soon-

to-be-middle-aged sexuality to wilt. Dashing
stranger lured you away till five AM.
Each page I turned, instead of heaving
the book, I took a step across the bridge.

Evan slept in my arms, his curls wild,
cheeks warm pink. Years later a friend
asked how I healed, how I got the old
inner ear gyroscope, the old ankle

flex balance. Evan slept. I turned
the pages instead of heaving
the book and said, Healing
is the wrong question. There are only steps

across the bridge that twisted, corkscrewed,
whipsawed, pitched, warped,
heaved behind me while Evan
slept, his breath warm on my neck.

Tit and tat

"Female African clawed frogs, when injected with the urine
of a pregnant woman, lay eggs within a few hours."

Elizabeth Kolberg, *The Sixth Extinction*

No one has injected a woman with African
clawed frog eggs (or frog pee) to test the inverse.
The panel that OK's human experiments
gets skittish when they hear "pregnant."

Reciprocals are proof in the calm
of a geometer's book-paneled study.
In the wild, x might very well equal
y, but don't bet your boots that y equals x.

The early worm does not get the bird.
Insubordinates on the food chain
are not model citizens. In fact, history
refers to them as "lunch." Children

who insist on fairness morph into adults
who like to acquire. We have nothing
to trade. You keep your tit. My tat
is folded compact in my lap.

On tombs

When the realtor showed me the land,
I missed the tombstones. Stupid, I know.
The oddly winding road looked quaint.

In the union hall I didn't notice every carpenter
was missing face parts, wore bloody coveralls,
walked with a drag-foot shuffle.

The architect promised Victorian gingerbread. Turrets
and spires. Monsard roofs and gables. Wraparound
porch. Space for the whole fam damily, plus inlaws.

What the contractor constructed, on the other
hand, was cramped, marble, windowless. The name
on the door is a nice touch, but we aren't that vain.

Quarter hourly chimes charmed the first day,
then got annoying. Maybe this is a clockless zone.
Maybe the constant clang explains solid construction.

It's a snug home. Every room is a bedroom
with space for nothing but a single bed. The builder
omitted commode, microwave, TV, fireplace.

Every weekend there are black-clad crowds.
They gather closer-clustered than American social
custom usually allows. Plus, no booze, or even Coke.

I want to meet the neighbors, but they only
emerge after dark. They stand still and stiff
on their marble houses and speak in semaphors.

What does two arms up mean? What does left
arm straight, right arm bent mean? Why do their hands
glow, and who is the reader of this odd text?

1918 flu epidemic

Dug no trenches but killed as many people
as World War I. Shot no machine guns.
Wore no round helmets. No germs with sharp
creased uniforms used wall maps and wooden
pointers to indicate attack. No homesick,
hand-rolled cigarette smoking infantry germ
wrote letters to sweethearts that got scissored
by censors. Germs did not convert their tractor
manufacturing plants to tank production.
Egghead germs did not encrypt and decrypt.
But they filled crypts. And acres of lawn. And ash-urns.

Why bother with bayonets? Why conscript
a farmer and leave a widow worried
about a field of rotting artichokes? Why print
ration books and conjure beef and butter
black markets? If you can't do better than a dude
one thousandth the size of a human cell, rethink.
Go back to making noodles. Return to teaching
three-year-olds the alphabet, teaching eight-
year-olds the art of paper airplane foldery,
teaching fifteen-year-olds rat anatomy.
Resume grafting apple branches. Do what you're
good at, and leave killing to the virus.

Before disaster

On her kitchen counter, tea leaves swirl in almost-boiling
water, impatient to settle, to signify menace with their ominous
cross-hatch, but she has walked away from her tea cup.

Fortune cookie fortunes, faux wisdom of the East,
abandon their cheerful sagacity and announce danger.
But the folded cookies are stale. She will dump them soon.

On her bookcase, Death and Hanged Man elbow their way
to the top of the silk-swaddle Tarot deck. She hasn't touched
Tarot cards since her wind-swept teen years.

On the shelf below, the Ouija board planchette
jitters across the alphabet, issuing stark warnings
in Ouija creole. She thinks the noise is a cricket.

Zodiac charts, I-Ching sticks, all the forecast apparatus,
all the portent machines, are eager to signal risk.
They are bursting from their boxes to be first

with bad news. Soon the phone will ring,
and a strange voice will stutter her name,
advise her to sit down, and announce

catastrophe. As if a chair could assuage shock!
The lines on her palm are already etched
with peril. But no one reads her own hand.

Every day every American pumps

"Every day, every American pumps, in effect, seven pounds of
carbon into the sea."

Elizabeth Kolberg, *The sixth extinction.*

The weight of a cat. Grandpa tossed
sack of unwanted kittens into the farm
pond. Grandpa was callous-hearted,

had to be to survive his rugged life.
But you, you must catch one semi feral
alley cat a day to heave in the ocean.

Don't find a semi feral by sundown,
you have to snatch a cat from the back
porch of the dementia-numbed lady

who counts her comfort in cats.
If the porch snatch fails, grab someone's
precious pet. Someone's Youtube champ.

Someone's lap-heat. Grandpa
chose to drown kittens he couldn't
feed. You, you are obligated.

The return of the bygones

It's homecoming weekend for bygones.
They chartered busses from surrounding cities.
My how you've grown. You're a full grown grudge!

They pump hands, thump each other's shoulders,
mutter macho nothings like *Let's do this thing.*
I'm the one they'll do it to. The guest of honor, oh boy.

Festering scads of bygones. Droves. Hoards.
The on and onslaught. Even the slightest
slight survived and thrived in exile.

Life flashes before my eyes.
I don't die, and it keeps flashing.
Memory lane is a superhighway

with a ten percent downgrade
and no shoulder. Trucks use low gear
says the sign but it's too late.

Bygones have a homing instinct like upstream-
scrambling salmon. Like passenger
pigeons. Like San Capistrano monarch butterflies.

No one knows when the next reunion is
or who's the next guest of honor. But busses
are easy to charter. My advice: clean up your trash.

Weight of the soul

Dr. McDougal claims a soul's weight
matches a bottle cap's. (What you scrape
from a lint trap after the tenth washing
of a flannel night gown. Four paperclips.
A pencil eraser. A baby tooth.
A shelled peanut. A cicada husk.)

Faith's defenders welcome
proof of soul. At last the atheistic hecklers
will be silenced. (Two sheets of paper.
A gobbet of bacon grease.) But on reflection,
sadness sets in. They'd hoped the soul
had more heft. After a life of prayer,
blisters from the long walk, scratches
from the thorn bushes that over-
lean the narrow path, a soul
should accumulate as much mass
as an apple, or a pocket New Testament,
gravity you can feel in your hands.

Atheistic hecklers are quick with ridicule.
That's no soul, they chuckle. That's a moment-
of-death belch and a trickle of spittle.
(A week's growth of toenails. Half a crouton.
Three blue jay feathers. A pinch of sand.)

Further tests are planned.
Does a churchgoer's soul have more
density than a surly sinner's? Is a genius's
soul heavier than a dullard's?
Or is each soul the same? (Three inches
of twine. Six tears. A pumpkin seed.)

Mountaintop removal

All fifty-three fourteen-thousand-foot peaks
in Colorado are clipped to nine thousand.
They are still fondly called fourteeners.

Every president on Mount Rushmore has a buzz
cut. Washington and Jefferson, diswigged. Lincoln's
notorious thatch, shorn. Roosevelt's bristle, pruned.

The same decree that renamed McKinley
Denali OK'ed altitude truncation.
Climbers no longer need oxygen tanks.

The Sierras are now a modest berm
dividing California's fertile Central Valley
and the scrubby Nevada desert.

Mount Katahdin, proud terminus
of the Appalachian Trail, is now Mound Katahdin.
You can climb it barefoot in ten minutes.

The Army Corps of Engineers explains: *A mountain
is a jewel box, a treasure chest, a bank vault.
We popped all the clasps to aid wildcat prospectors.*

Now claustrophobes can mine. No more canaries
needed. Mining is a weekend hobby. Every Army
Corps project has one lie at its heart.

The mountaintop removal spec book is missing
the ichthyological footnote. The creeks that trickled
from those blasted mountaintops still run clean, right?

What boys destroy

When I was four I dropped baby Gloria
head down and said, Mom, Glory fell.
Ninth birthday, I dangled my new GI Joe

action figure from the basement water
pipe and pocked it with my new BB gun.
Christmas when I was ten, my Swiss uncle sent

hand-made marionettes. They were trashed
before noon, fighting with BB-pocked GI Joe.
I torched bugs with a magnifying glass in sunlight,

with jumbled kill-lust and remorse. Die sorry die
sorry. My karma was corroded before puberty.
We won't discuss teen excesses and deficits.

I'll leave this bar soon, drive to the coast,
adopt a dog, find a tennis ball. Alcoholic
paralysis is penance in drag. The honor

plate in the skull hardens last. Conscience
is a wave that breaks over the feet of a man
throwing balls into surf for a loving dog.

Debt to society

I demand a receipt. I want my four cents change
in nickels. I pay my debt to society with a kited
check. I pay with Italian liras and want the payment
credited in Turkish liras. I pay with plastic, and pay
off that plastic with more plastic. I pay my debt in defunct
currency of a bankrupt state. I pay with wooden
nickels and plastic pennies, tiddlywinks and poker
chips. I pay with penny stocks, junk bonds
and war bonds. I pay with an IOU,
with an ee-i-ee-i-o. I pay with dot com bubble
gum. With a wheel of sharp cheddar, a wheel
of fortune, a soldier of fortune's life insurance.
I pay in Irish famine potatoes, in tulip mania
florins, fluoride tablets, placebos, blank checks,
voided checks, checkers, Parcheesi pieces. Why
are game pieces called men? You can run around that board,
collect two hundred dollars every time, but you still
are a boot, an iron, a thimble. The company pays
for me. The half life of a corporate conscience
is bankruptcy. I pay in tenths of a cent, a special
coin devised for gas pumps. I pump froth
into the economy. I pay with bit coin, with PayPal,
dots and dashes, sackcloth and ashes.
I'm not a deadbeat dad. Dad, can I borrow a few
bucks? Daddy Warbucks made me sing for my supper.
I owe society nothing. We're even. We're square.

Commencement

The kazoo master exceeds his toy's range,
gets bumped up to trumpet. It's like Louie Armstrong
came back, say the jazzhounds.

The accordion aficionado drops squeezebox
on curb, saunters into concert hall. He sits
at the grand piano. He knows how to sweep
coat tails out of the way. His glissando
brings tears to the classical
world's jaded snoots' eyes.

The ukulele prodigy grabs a hand
crafted classical guitar. Arpeggios
tumble from her fingers like water.

A lap-plunk zitherist turns to the harp.
She inhales courage, embraces the big
hulk and tilts it toward her. Everyone
in the house understands why
angels are portrayed as harpists.

A kid who can toot a tune on slide whistle
is halfway to trombone perfection.

A five gallon bucket thumper
is weeks from promotion to timpani.

A commencement ceremony marks
the switch from toy to instrument.
The works. Beribboned robes and tossed
mortarboards. Valedictorian. You are the future blah
blah carpe diem blah blah. Name called. Hand shaken.
Diploma given. Photo taken. Congratulations.

American history

We're great, granted. But kids, listen
to why. No other country's map so perfectly
fits a sheet of printer paper. The ancient
Greeks called it the Golden Rectangle. Ask

your math teacher. The Boston Tea
Partiers, Paul Revere on his nocturnal
horse whip, the Signers with their quills,
aren't content as satellite to so-called

great power Britain. What shape, what kind
of life is that? The so-called great power
is a wobbly triangle. Absurd to pay tea
taxes to the a wobbly triangle's

monarch. We ax the tea tax, nyah
-nyah-nyah King Triangle. We aren't content
to be a coastal squiggle perched on continent's
edge. So we march west.

Get out of our way, Spain, you old
-world square! We dream an empty
continent and slaughter the residents to make
dream fact. Another fact: the civil war

is a war of shape. Lincoln abhors slavery
but his real beef is the South slashes
our rectangle before it's rectagulated.
Gold rush, Californ-i-ay, bingo, mission

accomplished, manifestiny. Perfect
printer paper size. Of thee I sing.
Sea to shining sea. U.S.A.
Don't let anyone take it away.

Bunnies fake and real

Peter Rabbit is a watercolor fabricated in Beatrix
Potter's mind, with Flopsy et cetera and Mr.
McGregor who used to give you nightmares.

The Playboy bunny is fiction. Airbrushed to jerk-
worthy curviness. If that's your date threshold when you
start dating, every human will disappoint.

A jackalope is made up by Wyoming Souvenirs Inc
to fill gas station postcard racks. Because no landscape
between Cheyenne and the Tetons is worth the ink.

Easter B, March Hare, and Bugs, all fake fake fake.
Faker than the tooth fairy who at least traded nickels
for buds of enamel. Those dudes have nothing to parlay.

But dust bunnies are real as a snow boot. Reach your rag
under that bed. Indoor tumbleweed. Ethereal hairballs.
Proof you haven't cleaned your room
since you lost your baby teeth.

Kill Lazarus

Kill the troublemaker who siphons borderline
allegiants from the crowd's edge: always
the elite's first and last resort. It's Technique
One in the insurgence control handbook.

But this guy's *been* croaked. First croak didn't stick.
Do you think he'll do you the favor of staying
offed? If he dies five times, revivifies five
times, will you repeat the courtroom drama,

witness, bailiff, gavel, one more sentence,
one more kill? You'll feel silly. And what about
the squabble with the executioners' union?
You argue for a discount on same-dude

repeat executions. The union rep demands time
and a half to do in a guy who won't stay done in.
You can rehash the Kill Lazarus chatter all you want—
no one gets axed till you pass that impasse.

Fourth orbit

I would give you a zoo

I would give you a zoo with all nine maintenance
sheds, a gas pump gasket factory, a distillery
with its oak barrel scrubbing apparatus.

But I don't own those. I'd give you a whole suburban
strip mall Hallmark store, with anniversary cards
for all ethnicities and dog lovers' mugs.
But I own no Hallmark store, no retail real estate

of any kind. So pick what you want from all my stuff.
The chocolate milk stained clip-on bow tie: Yours.
The pants clips from my cycling days: Yours.
The drawerful of mismatched plastic flatware: Yours.
The lint collection sorted by shades of gray: Yours.

Help yourself to the chipped leprechaun statuette,
the one-legged egg beater. Grab the warped
mandolin fretboard, the crumpled kite string spool,
the swaybacked ironing board. Take a memento,
souvenir, keepsake, so when I'm in my balloon basket
over Bali, and you're back here in your comfy
kitchen, my heart will beat in your pickle jar.

When my father died it was like a whole library burned to the ground

Dad's last heart attack grips while he leans
his bike in front of the library. In the reference
stacks, sparks smolder among almanacs and atlases.
The reference librarian grabs the phone
and answers a question about poisonous
mushrooms. His other hand points English-
Spanish dictionary readers toward the exit.

Dad's range collapses: a mile, a block, a hall.
Magazines, both frequently thumbed
and never consulted, ignite with a soft
puff. The periodicals manager swings the fire
door closed as sprinklers turn ashes to mush.

Dad curses his morning stack of pills.
With every swallow an I-can-read-it-myself
book explodes in the children's room.
The story-time volunteer leads children,
double file, hold hands, to the lawn.

Botched surgery leaves a cow heart
valve lodged in Dad's aorta, downstream
of his abdomen. Surgeons assure it will
do no harm. The bill is high enough

to deny guilt, low enough to discourage
a lawsuit. The check-out desk clerk
waives fines for a worried patron.

Dad tumbles on the treadmill test. The local history
room smoke-blackens. Dad never tries the new
wheelchair. He only sticks the oxygen
tubes in his nostrils when dizziness heaves him.

The used book store volunteer scans
new arrivals he might want to snag
and taps the doorknob for heat.
He murmurs to browsers, "It's time to go."

The head librarian, at the Can I Help You desk,
slips a new library card form onto a clipboard
and picks up the five-year-old who just learned
to sign her name. "We'll finish this outside," she says.
Dad brings his books to check out. The new
librarian, first day on the job, smiles as she handles
Dad's choices. She's too discreet to say,
but they're all on her must-read list.

On his last day, the nurse says, "Tomorrow
we'll move you to Assisted Living." Dad holds
up the pile of novels, new novels by his favorite
authors, paperbacks, mothwings of ash. "This,"
he says, "this is the assistance I need."

When a man greets you
as a serpent

The dude is snake spooked. He's constrictor
afflicted. He stared into the poison-sac-
equipped gullet of a real or imagined
beast and freaked out. It's not about you.

Perhaps he squeezed foot into boot and an asp
snapped at his heel. Or a boa constrictor
snatched his baby, encoiling the infant
while sidewinding twenty miles an hour

on the gravel road to the swamp. Stop. Wait.
Maybe it is you. You make a living selling snake
oil cure-all to the gullible. Your clients are the cancer-
laced, the gout-grumpy, the victim of falling
anvil whose hip won't heal. The guy bought
a bottle for his ailing mother to stanch her ache.
She died. And here you are, with your snake-
skin wingtip shoes. You can't revive

his dear mommy. But you can say sorry.
You can say you're really, really sorry.
Give the chump back his buck. Dump
your stash in the trash and exit.

On wings

Take a nickel. Take every nickel in my pocket.
Take a cigarette or carton. Take a bus token
or all-day bus pass. I'll loan you my cheap
tux for your glitzy shindig. You can borrow

my beat-up pickup to haul trash.
But when I grew these wings
I vowed I'd keep them on my back.
My wings were cultured from cheek

swabbed tissue. My cheek. My wings
might be designed with a homing instinct.
They might deliver you crashing
through my bedroom window. Might

end our friendship. If your antibodies
kick in at ten thousand feet and reject
the appendages, you plummet. If
you are predisposed to molt in thin

atmosphere (how would you know?),
it's plummet time again. There are etiquette
questions. In a restaurant, can you fold
wings into a suit jacket so you don't block

a waiter's path? Can you stand in a crowded
subway car without obstructing the door?
Think of the legal complexities. If you collide
with a plane, am I loss-of-life liable?

Will your heirs sue me if you're bazooka'ed
in a no-fly zone? Deuteronomy says, Covet not
thy neighbor's body parts. Kindergarten teachers
say, You get what you get, and you don't get upset.

I got condor wings, designed for riding updrafts.
You got penguin wings, destined for ridicule.
I don't understand cosmic inequality. I just know:
No, you can't borrow my wings.

Piñata in the marching band

You don't re-origamify an inflated airbag
and stuff it into its pouch with hope
it repeats its trick next crash.

You don't want a condom
rolled off the slick cock
and stuffed into its envelope.

These are one-use items,
and no one complains, even in this stern
reduce / reuse / recycle climate.

So get off my back about the piñata.
A bee dies in the sting, and a male
praying mantis is only good for one screw

before the female snacks on his head.
At most hysterical tune's climax,
in front of the judges' booth, the bass

drums do their thing, the low note
of a baritone sax makes everyone pride-
giddy. The drum major will nod at me.

I will deliver a resolute whack that ricochets
for city blocks. It's a thump no
drum can muster plus candy.

On sincerity

When I crush a heart with my body,
I say to it in my seeds, your apple
shall live in my teeth. No that's wrong.

When I crush a body with my apple,
I say to it in my teeth, your heart
shall live in my seeds. No that's wrong.

I try to speak the simple truth, Kahlil,
But kinks dominate. Runners and tendrils
run and tend to complicate. Left footnotes

multiply and flatulate. Flattery asks
who to congratulate. Verbs get conjugal
and conjugate. Nouns ask, "Now what?"

I instruct my heart to earnestly serenade
the apple before my teeth do the deed
they were sharpened for, but heart

must borrow larynx from snarky
brain. How can an organ called a larynx
refrain from back-talk? Every move

is a sarcasm spasm, call and response,
catch and release, flint and spark,
insult self-smitten in the dark.

Minor neurosurgery

We're gonna disconnect the thingy in the language
zone from the sensory doodad that's pressing
on your, you know, think-muscle. Shrink
the autonomic whatsit with a laser beam
because it's getting too big for its little brain-
britches. Then cauterize the memory doohickey,
bolt your lid back on and send you home.

Questions before we start. If you die before you wake,
it's my fault, true or false? If you almost die, would you
rather be a root vegetable or leafy salad vegetable,
or should we leave you in the parking lot and let
nature have its way? What is your faith? What's
your guardian angel's faith? Lastly, who loves
you enough to pay for this six-figure procedure?

You'll be awake during surgery. If you want ear-
plugs to blunt the skull-saw sound, ask.
Pop quiz! How many flingers am I upholding?
Who's the president of Arkansas? Do you have cavities
or caveats? Count for me backward from one
hundred, but double every prime number and subtract
three from every square. What did you eat for lurch?

OK. All patched up. The surgery was a resousousou
sucsucsucsuc. You might feel a twinge of pain,
a ping of pain, a ping pong popdog, a poodle of pain.
Take a painkiller. Assassin of assassins. We need
to hurry up you out of here. The suture surgeon
will stitch while you credit your hand card
to the nice people of the billing department. Ta ta.

The triumph of pipsqueak hellions

I learned my social and language skills eighth
grade back of the class where the jackasses
sat. We were masters of caustic, tuned
like a hound's snout to the chance for caricature.

We crafted our own slang, insult
stacked on quip. A whiff of a ridiculee's weakness
was whipped into grotesque meringue. A dude's
only hope of cool: laugh when laughed at.

This was the year of full bloom brilliance,
grace still unsprouted. We were pubescent
bulls in a china shop. China shop? No, sir, a pile
of porcelain chips when we swaggered in.

Six, fifty-minute periods a day. One hundred eighty
school days. That's over a thousand chances
for a teacher to puncture that funky cloud of hormones,
snark, and princely rage. Actual punctures: nil.

Teachers caucused often to weigh expel, detain, whip
and (fantasy) firing squad. We crossed unbroken
to adolescence because the school manual didn't list hard
labor, and no one picked up when school phoned home.

Life is too short for mediocre hot dogs

(Sign on a gas pump, 2016)

My death bed regrets: I didn't chase my son
when he stomped out of my third wedding.
I left that unicycle leaning in the garage unridden.
Never shook hands with Ernest Hemingway.

I didn't stop for a gas station hot dog.
A hot dog is so-so by definition, I thought.
So I topped off my tank and drove off.
Now, body cancer-laced, one lung left,

hours to live, I wish I'd walked
into that gas station and said,
"Give me one of your better-than-mediocre
dogs." My son's a thousand miles

away. The unicycle will get sold, estate
sale. No one writes like Hemingway. I'll never
eat solid food again, with or without nitrates.
If I'd eaten that hot dog, I could die happy.

Between

When you get that magic static radio
crackle, don't spin the dial.
You're in a place where weirdness prevails

in a good way. Static scratches an ancient itch.
The stretch of road where one signal
fails and another comes in faint is wild

land. Stop. Look around. You'll find weeds
that grow nowhere else. The people who run
convenience stores care about your convenience.

They remember being kids and give candies to kids.
They remember hitchhiking and offer coffee, no
charge, to hitchhikers. On your second visit,

even if it's a year later, they'll recall if
you are the Ho Hos type or the MoonPies.
Kids who lives in radio boundaries learn foreign

languages fast. Most are ambidextrous.
Residents show up for meetings
of the school board or county council

with no gripe—just to listen. Churches
have signs out front that say All are welcome—
like churches everywhere. But these churches

really welcome. Pastors ask your beliefs
and laugh about their own. Plan your next trip
so you can join the ministers at their weekly

meeting. Egg salad sandwiches.
Straight laced to gush-clap
to backslid, you never heard so much laughing.

Rockwell's lamppost

Rockwell aimed his brain at an imaginary lamp-
post each Tuesday evening to conjure a Saturday
Evening Post cover. With lamppost fixed in head,
he built a scene around it (disheveled

paperboy heaves too-heavy load, pack
of mutts chase meat truck, church-choir
soprano soloist warms her warble).
Then remove the lamppost, and presto!

small town Americana delivered
with a chuckle. My technique is reverse
Rockwell. I start with a lamppostless canvass
and fill in gold delicious apples in a red

bowl, stormy seascape with looming cliffs,
what have you. The lamppost is the final
flourish. My best works: poppy field,
Alpenglow background, lamppost foreground.

Cowboys horseback lassoing dogeys. Moon
rising over sage-scattered mesas. Lonely
lamppost on horizon. Now I dabble in abstract.
Raw color splash, muscular geometry.

Soon I'll go full Pollock, random splatter,
meaning, meaningless, lamppost, inverse J,
jaywalking across whatever new schools
of art nonsense sprout in this post-millenial century.

Late for the party

God couldn't decide what bangles to wear
to the big bang and came one minute late.
Or, God's zoot suited broad shoulders got stuck
in a worm hole short cut en route. Or, God took
the wrong bus and detoured toward apocalypse
instead of coming straight to the emergence
of everything from a gift wrapped box of nothing.

Whatever reason, no excuse, God was sixty
seconds late. God is kicking the supreme self
for missing the moment the all-cuisine
cookbook was legible. The moment the twelve
church choirs assigned to the twelve dimensions
sang warm up scales. The moment a person
could pluck the cables connecting effect, side
effect, collateral damage, and friendly fire.
The moment the pop rocks of all matter started
to sizzle, plus non matter and antimatter.

Things got started without the big blessing.
We stumble through the universe,
luminous and human brushing shoulders
against each other, talking, talking, talking.
Why is nature cruel? God says, Beats me.
How will it end? God says, Big shrug.
Who's in charge? God says.
I could have been God.

Hall pass

All I need is that signed pink paper square
to float in the corridor alone with the light
that slants through wire-meshed windows.

No bullies elbow me into lockers. The bullies
sit bored in the backs of classrooms, or smear
a waxy sheen of deodorant in their pits

after PE or wait in the outer office till the assistant
principal calls them for the ultimate ultimatum
or slip out the side door. Fuck it. Hooky.

Smart kids shuffle modestly toward teachers'
desks. They doublechecked their answers
while they read the quiz questions.

In the music room, the recorder orchestra
tortures Aunt Rhodie, flat, not a single
student pushing enough air through the little

wood pipe to hold the dirge aloft. In every
classroom I pass, teachers gesture, poking
info into the heads of children. I walk the length

of scuffed linoleum, free as a rabbit in a meadow
with no foxes, no hawks. The clapper keeps—ten
more minutes—a respectful distance from the bell.

Hobo's lullaby

No cops in heaven, imagine.
No night shift, day shift, no billy club,
no black jack. No itch
to toss you into a paddy wagon.

Judge? Sure. Empty courtroom,
law books open to the v-for-vagrancy page.

Prosecutor in fancy suit waits
for phone to ring, courier to knock,
secretary to deliver indictment.
Meanwhile he practices—for millennia—
his anti-loitering palaver,
his, "Ladies and gentlemen of the jury."

The defense attorney, court-appointed, cheap
skirt and blazer, well slept
and underworked. Those piles of files
on her desk? Ideas for novels. Imagine.

Heaven's jailer oversees thousands
of empty cells. He's adept at banging
on the bars, calls it vertical vibraphone. Hear
chimes in a thunderstorm? Now you know.

Jailhouse cafeteria is inmateless, but they keep
slapping together bologna sandwiches,
keep ladling thin broth, one bean per bowl.
If you visit a church basement soup kitchen
where there is no sermon-before-supper
rule, that's heaven-surplus food.
That's proof heaven has no cops.

Don't host despair

Despair is not a guest. The difference
between a house guest and a sneak thief:
arsenicked watchdogs. Kitchen door window
pane shattered. No guest would greet
you pocket bulging with pearls, your pearls.
No bona fide guest arrives with pistol
in pocket. Of course, he said he never
shoots. That's what all sneak thieves say,
believe before the caper goes south.

Give Despair the ultimatum, talking to, heave
ho. The boot. We need the guest room ready
for Miss Felicity, who gets here who knows
when. Fluff pillows! Beat rugs! Swipe
cobwebs! Banish dust bunnies! Miss
Felicity is / might be / probably is / why not
lifting the door knocker now. Miss Felicity travels
with an entourage. She's a houseful of guest
and requires a host's whole hospitality.

Celebration of pop-up things

Bless toast and prairie dogs! All hail Jack
in his box! Crank turns, monkey and weasel
plunk. POP! The toddler chortles. Praise prank
springs snake-coiled in fake nut cans.

Honor Old Faithful and her sibling geysers
that squirt for patient tourists' cameras.
Hurray for toy rockets with their parent-
scaring warnings. I love pebbles in sling

shots in the hands of a circle of kids
on their backs. I adore gazpacho in a lidless
blender and its ceiling Rorschach. Yay
for the cheap straw boater hat that pops

off in a bluster and takes a toupee with it.
The trophy, the grand prize, the A-1 popper,
is the pop-up book. In kindergarten,
I had just mastered letters and words,

page turn without tear, when I opened
a pop-up book. Paper that mimics
the gymnastic thrust of muscle, cartilage,
and joints. Origami turning cartwheels.

Karma's not a bitch

It gives karma no pleasure to bring
the bug-crusher back as a bug. Karma
does not relish her disciplinary role.

You chose your own fate. Karma just
wrote in her notebook. You
magnified sunlight and scorched

a beetle's carapace. You trampled an ant
hill. You tore all six legs off dozens of bugs.
There was that time you thought

you were a friend of trusting fireflies,
but you punched no holes in the jar lid,
and they choked on each other's stale

exhale. Karma's not a bitch. Not a sadist.
Not a disciplinarian. This is not revenge.
"This hurts me more than it hurts

you," says Karma as she squirts you
from oblivion's tube into the clatter
and kaleidoscope of insect life.

Charles Darwin in Eden

The Beagle spins in a storm coming home
from the Galapagos and beaches
in Eden Bay. Adam sits at his desk.
A parade of birds marches past.

"Finch," says Adam. He writes finch
in his ledger. "Finch, finch, finch."
"Why do you call them all finches?"
Darwin asks. "It's the sound of their rustle

in the branches," answered Adam.
"Each finch beak fits a different flower,"
says Darwin. "It proves natural selection."
Adam says, "I thought they were all just finches."

Darwin worries, "I don't wish to offend
your faith, sir." Adam counters, "I'm sorry
I can't help with your research." Eve drifted
across the sand and wades hip deep

into the ocean. She lifts her arms,
and unnamed finches settle on her fingers.
"Delightful lady, delightful,"
Darwin murmurs. Adam agrees.

Gloat picnic

The bully crushed my foot and his Batman lunch
box clasp unhitched. His marshmallow fluff
on Wonderbread sandwich fell to the corrugated
grime of the school bus floor.

That was 8 AM. Now it's noon.

> The bully watches angels unfold a linen
> tablecloth, still warm from heaven's iron,
> bleached to blinding sun-catch. The bully's
> hungry but proud, too cruelty-cornered
> to admit he wants to come to my picnic.

The homeroom sub called me Samson
instead of Sam. The class guffawed.
I corrected her calmly. She said, Don't
shout. I shouted OK. Five demerits.

That was 9 AM. Now it's noon.

> Her cell phone died, so she can't tell
> her boyfriend where to bring the leftover
> spaghetti she left on the porch railing.
> She's hungry but is sure angels
> are mythical. She can't stop staring
> as they unpack the picnic basket.

The math teacher said, Do Better, as he dropped
my quiz (40% correct) on my desk. Dividing
fractions is dumb. Only dumb people do it.

That was 10. Now it's noon.

> The math teacher watches out the teachers'
> lounge window. He wishes he'd asked
> me to meet at lunch, divide fractions
> together, share his stale pizza.

The girl who thinks I have a crush
on her (I don't) flew a hate note paper
airplane into my back pack and giggled
with her friends when I read it.

That was 11. Now it's noon.

> Yes I threw her lunch sack into the tree, which
> she deserved. No, I won't share my lunch
> with her. She would think I liked her.

An angel dips a spoon in heaven honey.
Another breaks open a heaven croissant.
Strawberries roll in a bowl of powdered
sugar. Sweet peppers every hue
from blood to sunshine. I am glutted.
My enemies are hungry.
Forever and ever.
Amen.

Origins

13   Queen Victoria's reading list: Franklee Gilbert,
Little known contributors to mathematics.
"Queen Victoria liked Alice in Wonderland so
much that she wrote to Carroll and asked him
for the rest of his works. With his humble duty,
C. L. Dodgson presented Her Majesty with
a number of volumes, all mathematical, and
including a treatise on The Condensation of
Determinants."

22   Heaven forbids me to be proud and
presumptuous. The title is a quote from Boris
Pasternak, explaining to the Soviet Writers
Union why he accepted the Nobel Prize in
Literature in spite of their objections

23   Family of saints: Rosemary Ellen Guilley, *The
Encyclopedia of Saints.* "Adalbald fell in love
with Rictude (later sainted herself). They had
four children: St. Maurontius, St. Clotsindis,

St. Eusebia, St. Adalsindis)."

25   Show and tell: Louise Erdrich, *The Round house*. "Not everyone has a monster and most who do keep it locked up."

35   On nudity: Kahlil Gibran, *The Prophet*. "Tear off your garment yet leave it in no man's path."

46   The oozers against the tidies: Kay Ryan introucing one of her poems at a reading. "I'm not one of the body fluid poets."

48   The lost boy: JM Barrie, *Peter Pan*. "John's [Neverland] had a lagoon with flamingos flying over it … while Michael, who was very small, had a flamingo with lagoons flying over it."

50   On witnesses: Kahlil Gibran, *The Prophet*. "Know that all the blessed dead are standing among you and watching."

51   When the unclean spirit leaves a man: *The Gospel of Matthew, 12: 43-45*. "It passes through waterless places seeking rest, and does not find it. Then it says, 'I will return to my house from which I came'; and when it comes, it finds it unoccupied, swept, and put in order. Then it goes and takes along with it seven other spirits more wicked than itself, and they go in and live there."

55   Brain facts: Steven Pinker, *How the Mind Works*. "An average adult knows the names of

about ten thousand things. Even the average six year old knows a few thousand."

63 On tombs: Kahlil Gibran, *The Prophet.* "You shall not dwell in tombs made by the dead for the living."

69 Weight of the soul: Duncan McDougal, *Hypothesis concerning soul substance together with experimental evidence of the the existence of such substance.* "He expired and suddenly coincident with death the beam end dropped with an audible stroke hitting against the lower limiting bar and remaining there with no rebound. The loss was ascertained to be three-fourths of an ounce."

80 Kill Lazarus: *The Gospel of John, 12:10-11.* "So the chief priests made plans to kill Lazarus as well, for on account of him many of the Jews were deserting them and believing in Jesus."

83 When my father died it was like a whole library burned to the ground: Laurie Anderson, *World Without End.*

85 When a man greets you as a serpent: Charles Dickens, *The Pickwick Papers.* "When you have parted with a man at two o'clock in the morning on terms of upmost good fellowship, and he meets you again at eight and greets you

as a serpent, it is not unreasonable to conclude that something of an unpleasant nature has occurred meanwhile."

86   On wings: Kahlil Gibran, *The Prophet*. "The vision of one man lends not its wings to another man."

89   On sincerity: Kahlil Gibran, *The Prophet*. "When you crush an apple with your teeth, say to it in your heart, your seeds shall live in my body."

99   Hobo's lullaby: Woody Guthrie, *Hobo's Lullaby*. "When you die and go to heaven you won't find no police there."

101   Don't host despair: Janet Fitch, *White Oleander*. "I wanted to tell her not to entertain despair. Despair wasn't a guest. You didn't play its favorite music, find it a comfortable chair. Despair is the enemy."

105   Gloat picnic: *Psalm 23*. "Thou hast prepared a table before me in the presence of mine enemies."